Two Purple Gloves
A comedy
Michael Park

New Theatre Publications - London
www.plays4theatre.com

The edition published in 2013

New Theatre Publications

2 Hereford Close | Warrington | Cheshire | WA1 4HR | 01925 485605

www.plays4theatre.com   email: info@plays4theatre.com

New Theatre Publications is the trading name of the publishing house that is owned by members of the Playwrights' Co-operative. This innovative project was launched on the 1st October 1997 by writers Paul Beard and Ian Hornby with the aim of encouraging the writing and promotion of the very best in New Theatre by Professional and Amateur writers for the Professional and Amateur Theatre at home and abroad.

ISBN 9 781 840 94927 8

Characters

Harry
Connie

Copyright Information

Video-Recording of Amateur Productions

Performing Licence Applications

A performing licence for these plays will be issued by "New Theatre Publications" subject to the following conditions.

Conditions

1. That the performance fee is paid in full on the date of application for a licence.
2. That the name of the author(s) is/are clearly shown in any programme or publicity material.
3. That the author(s) is/are entitled to receive two complimentary tickets to see his/her/their work in performance if they so wish.
4. That a copy of the play is purchased from New Theatre Publications for each named speaking part and a minimum of three copies purchased for backstage use.
5. That a copy of any review be forwarded to New Theatre Publications.
6. That the New Theatre Publications logo is clearly shown on any publicity material. This is available on our website.

Fees

Details of script prices and fees payable for each performance or public reading can be obtained by telephone to (+44) 01925 485605 or to the address below.

Alternatively, latest prices can be obtained from our website www.plays4theatre.com where credit/debit cards can be used for payment.

To apply for a performing licence for any play please write to New Theatre Publications 2 Hereford Close, Warrington, Cheshire WA1 4HR or email info@plays4theatre.com with the following details:-

1. Name and address of theatre company.
2. Details of venue including seating capacity.
3. Dates of proposed performance or public reading.
4. Contact telephone number for Author's complimentary tickets.

Or apply directly via our website at www.plays4theatre.com

Two Purple Gloves
by Michael Park

Two Purple Gloves was first performed in the Scarborough Amateur
Drama festival at the YMCA Theatre, November 2001 with the following
cast:

Harry Hollingsworth. Arthur Holland
Connie Franklin. . . . . Susan Cremer

Directed by Arthur Holland

Characters

Harry Hollingsworth - 70, an out-of-work actor, reduced to sleeping
rough

Connie Franklin - 20s, a part-time security guard in a shopping mall

*The scene is part of an indoor shopping complex in the week before
Christmas. Two large signs hang to left and right of stage, or are
mounted left and right on proscenium arch, facing forward. One carries
the legend 'Stairs and Toilets' with an arrow, the other says 'Way Out to
Victoria Street' with an arrow. They can be garnished with Christmas
sparkle. Signs bearing the names of various High Street stores, including
a stationer's, are pinned to a black backcloth at rear. Slightly to L of
centre is a bench or a set of chairs placed to allow foot-weary shoppers
to rest awhile. DR is a small undecorated Christmas tree on a stand. UC
is a large municipal litterbin. The area around the bench should be
capable of being illuminated in colour for the finale. The opening music,
a cheerful Christmas carol, is played, and when the Curtain opens, the
stage is in darkness except for a faint overall green glow from the
(unseen) emergency exit lights. On the bench, Harry Hollingsworth is
lying with his back to the audience. He wears a disreputable light-
coloured mackintosh, an equally grubby felt hat, dark trousers and black
shoes. Two carrier bags containing all his worldly possessions are
resting against L end of the bench, and an empty wine bottle is on the
ground at R end. A mop and bucket are parked UL.*

*The music fades as Connie enters from stage right. She is young and
wears an ill–fitting uniform comprising tight black trousers, an overlarge
dark blouson, and black ankle boots. A badge attached to the jacket
carries her identification. She holds a walkie-talkie which is in direct radio
contact with Geoff, her (unseen) boss, who is located in an office
somewhere in the bowels of the building. Connie also carries a
rubberised torch, which she shines around. She speaks with a Northern
accent.*

Connie   Geoff? Geoff? Are you there, Geoff? Come on! Don't be such a pillock! Put some lights on, will you? It's as black as your hat down here. *(Pause.)* Come on! Hey, you haven't skived off to the bog, have you? *(Pleadingly.)* Don't muck me about. It's dead creepy down here. I keep seeing my torch reflected in the shop windows and it doesn't half make me jump, I can tell you! *(Pause.)* All right, I admit it, you've succeeded in scaring the pants off me. *(To herself.)* But don't think you're gonna get the chance to find out if that's true, matey! *(Louder.)* Will you be told? I need some light! Look, if I trip over something and break a leg, I'll crawl down to that office and bloody well kill you! And I'll sue your two-bit security firm for every penny it owns. *(Pause.)* Oh, all right, have it your own way. You have your bit of fun, Geoff Ryder. But don't blame me if I can't do my job. Don't come running to me when a major national clothing chain gets broken into because I haven't checked their locks. I'll just put it in my report - 'Unable to check security of premises in Tollerbay Shopping Centre on account of not being able to see a hand in front of my bloody face'! *(She slowly shines her torch around, the beam illuminating Harry on his bench. To herself.)* Hold on! What's this? *(Into radio.)* Geoff! Look, I'm not kidding now! I need some lights on - urgent! *(Suddenly, the stage is blindingly illuminated in white.)* Ha, ha! Very funny! I said *some* lights, not the whole sodding shooting match! It's like Blackpool Illuminations down here. And you've probably blinded me for life!

(The lights fade to a more acceptable glow. Connie switches the torch off and moves cautiously towards the bench. She bends down, picks up the bottle and sniffs it, grimaces, then puts it down again. She tiptoes to the other end of the bench and looks in the carrier bags. She moves to the bench and hesitates, unsure how to tackle the situation. Eventually, she reverses the torch and pokes Harry with the end of it. Harry moans and moves. Connie jumps back. Harry resumes sleeping. Connie returns and pokes him again. This time, Harry wakes up and struggles to sit up. Connie retreats to a safe distance. Harry, by nature, speaks slowly and precisely, enunciating every word clearly. This is compounded by his being slightly drunk, though he attempts to appear sober.)

Harry   Wha...? Whassamarrer? *(He rubs his eyes and sits up.)* Turn the lights out, will you? There's a good girl.

Connie   What do you think I am? Matron of an old folks' home? You shouldn't be in here.

Harry   What's the time?

Connie   Just after midnight.

Harry   Good grief! I've only just managed to get off to sleep!

Connie   You can't sleep here. In fact, you've no business here at all.

Harry   Young lady, correct me if I am in any way misinformed, but this is a shopping centre, is it not? True, it has a large roof overhead, *(He shields his eyes.)* and rather bright lighting. But, that apart, it is, I believe, still a street of shops, and thus intended for perambulating by members of the general public.

Connie   Well, yes, of course it is - at least if 'perambulating' is what I think it means. But only during opening hours. And late night shopping ended at ten.

Harry   For which I am truly grateful. I would never have been able to sleep had the general public still been stampeding around in here.

Connie   How did you get in here anyway? I locked the outer doors myself. And I know Geoff went round checking there was no one left behind.

Harry   Ah, a slight subterfuge was necessary there. Let us say that this Geoff isn't the most assiduous of searchers. In fact, despite my age and lack of mobility, I found it relatively easy to stay one jump ahead of him.

Connie   Yeah, well, that makes sense anyway. But it doesn't take away from the fact that I've caught you now. So you'll have to leave.

Harry   But it was raining outside earlier. Surely you wouldn't throw an old man out on a night like this?

Connie   Yeah… well… it's probably stopped now.

Harry   Oh, I doubt it. In fact, I believe the forecast said there was a distinct possibility of snow before the night was out. In any case, I'm ill.

Connie   Ill? You can probably put that down to the booze.

Harry   *(with great feeling).* I only drink to forget.

Connie   Forget what?

Harry   *(chuckling).* I've forgotten! I am *so* sorry, young lady. I just cannot resist adding in the old punchlines. It's the nature of my work.

Connie   Oh, you do work, do you? Some skilled job down the Council tip, perhaps?

Harry   Ah, how cruel the young can be these days! I blame it on all these free handouts. They don't know what it's like to fall on hard times.

Connie	Well, go and fall on your hard times somewhere else. Or would you rather I reported your presence to Geoff?
Harry	Would you say that this Geoff is a fit man?
Connie	He thinks he is.
Harry	And is he the type who is likely to resort to violence?
Connie	'Course he is! That's why he founded a security firm, so he could bash people about without being arrested for it.
Harry	*(standing)*. In that case, perhaps I had better... *(He puts a hand to his head and sways unsteadily.)* ...had better...
Connie	*(moving to him)*. Here, you're not really ill, are you? Oh, I get it! You're going for the sympathy vote! Well, forget it! I may be a woman, but I'm as tough as any man.
Harry	*(sitting)*. I'm sure you are. *(He sighs.)* That's the problem. No one has any time for anyone else these days – not even at Christmas, a season, so we are led to believe, of goodwill to all men.
Connie	Maybe, but I still have my job to do, even at Christmas... *especially* at Christmas. Did you know that this place becomes a happy hunting ground for tea-leafs?
Harry	Ah, you've just said the magic word. *(With relish.)* Tea! I don't suppose the kettle would happen to be boiling, would it?
Connie	*(laughing in disbelief)*. You've got a nerve! This isn't the Salvation Army, you know.
Harry	Tell me, would you happen to have the keys to these various retail outlets about your person?
Connie	*(suspicious)*. Why do you want to know?
Harry	I was just thinking that I might be able to get some meagre refreshment from yonder café. Is it a good place to eat?
Connie	I believe so. Why don't you come back when it's open and try it? Now, come on – *please*!
Harry	I will leave, I promise faithfully, just as soon as I regain total control of my legs.
Connie	Make it snappy, will you? I've got my rounds to do. I'm supposed to check every lock every hour, and there are a hell of a lot of locks in a place this size!
Harry	Please don't let me stop you.
Connie	I can't go off checking security while there's a dirty great hole in that security right in front of my eyes!
Harry	Look, I'll do a deal with you. What if I promise to sit right here, without moving a muscle, while you carry out your tasks?
Connie	*(cautiously)*. You won't go wandering about?

Harry   Where is there to go? I cannot obtain access to any of the shops, the outer door is, I presume, well and truly secured, and anyway, my legs seem to have given up the ghost for the moment.

Connie All right then. But you stay right there till I get back, OK?

Harry   *(raising three fingers to his brow).* Scout's honour.

Connie *(still hesitant).* Yeah… well… I shan't be long.

Harry   Take your time. In fact, take all night.

Connie I'm not doing that! You've only got a stay of execution, that's all.

Harry   You could have picked a less threatening metaphor.

Connie Right then. I'm off.

Harry   Farewell! And remember to take your time!
(Connie looks at him, then makes up her mind and crosses the stage to exit L. As soon as she has gone, Harry tips his hat over his eyes, pulls his coat about him, and lies down on the seat again, closing his eyes. He fidgets, then sits up, takes one of his carriers and ferrets inside. He pulls out some clothes, folds them into a pillow, and lies down again. He is happier with this arrangement, but the lights get in his eyes. He sits up again, looks in his carrier and takes out a broken pair of sunglasses. He perches these on his nose. He shivers, takes out an old, torn, coloured sheet and carefully lays it over himself. After some wriggling to find the best position, he finally snuggles down again. There is a brief pause, then Connie enters R. She is carrying a cardboard box containing Christmas tree decorations and fairy lights. She stops dead when she sees Harry. She shakes her head, then goes over, puts the box down near the tree, and wakes him.)

Harry   *(sitting up).* Tell me, have you ever thought of seeking employment as an alarm clock?

Connie *(laughing at the sunglasses).* Where do you think you are? South of France? And you were supposed to just sit there quietly, not kip down again!

Harry   *(taking off the sunglasses and putting them in his pocket).* Ah, would that I *were* in foreign parts, instead of having to endure another long, damp, cold English winter.

Connie You and me both. But we've got to face reality. And at the moment, you happen to be *my* reality.

Harry   Do you come across many of me in your work?

Connie One or two, but they're usually harmless. You get pretty good at sizing people up.

Harry	*(looking around).* Er, what, er, people?
Connie	I'm not always on the night shift. I do days as well. But I prefer nights, especially this time of year. During the day, it's like a fairground. But at night, walking around here, all alone, it feels like you're the only person left alive. Like you've been left in charge of the whole world. Well, at least this little bit of it.
Harry	What about, er, Geoff?
Connie	Him? He never strays far from that office. Once he's checked to see if everyone's out, you don't see him again till dawn. He's in charge of the monitors, you see.
Harry	You mean there are other people working for him beside you? Like milk monitors?
Connie	*(laughing). Television* monitors! There's CCTV all over this building. *(As he obviously doesn't understand.)* Closed circuit television cameras.
Harry	Everywhere?
Connie	S'right.
Harry	Even in the, er, facilities?
Connie	The what?
Harry	The washrooms.
Connie	*(laughing).* I don't think the owners have got round to spying in there yet. Anyway, they're all over the place in here.
Harry	Perhaps if you turned off the lights…?
Connie	That won't make any difference. They can pick up every detail, even in the dark. Infra-red, they are.
Harry	So you're saying that, at this very moment… *(He looks upwards.)* …we are being observed?
Connie	Highly unlikely. There just happens to be an ordinary colour tele' down there in the office too. Geoff'll be absorbed in the midnight movie. I doubt he's even noticed the monitors.
Harry	And you say there's no chance he'll be dropping in on us?
Connie	Hold on a minute! Don't you go getting any ideas! I do have a direct link to the police station.
Harry	But by the time you contacted them on your wireless there, I could have taken it off you.
Connie	I'd like to see you try, mate! There are concealed panic buttons all over the place.
Harry	You can relax. I've no wish to become involved with the forces of law and order.
Connie	Ah, been in trouble with them before, have you?
Harry	A simple case of mistaken identity.

Connie   Right. But just remember – one wrong move…

Harry   Sadly, I've been making the wrong moves most of my life. *(Pause.)* So, is all safely locked up?

Connie   Yeah. And it'd make my life a lot easier if you were too. Or at least, if you were well away from here. How are the legs? *(Harry takes off the sheet and tries to stand, but has to stretch out his arms to steady himself. Connie assists him to sit again.)* You know, I'm sure you're just putting this on.

Harry   Regrettably not. I really am not feeling steady on my feet yet. Incidentally, you haven't, er, reported my presence to this Geoff, have you?

Connie   'Course not. You're *my* responsibility. I'm not having him saying Connie Franklin can't cope. Oh, wouldn't he just love that! *(She speaks in a weak, 'girly' voice.)* Geoff, can you help me? I'm being threatened by a bloke old enough to be my grandfather. And he's so dangerous, he can't even stand up! *(Normal voice.)* Oh, he'd love to act the big macho male rescuing the damsel in distress – providing the movie he's watching hasn't reached an exciting bit. Only trouble is, if I did that, he'd never let me forget it. Look, I'll give you another ten minutes, and that's all! In fact, while you're recovering, you can help me with a small job.

Harry   I regret that the legs won't take to being employed in any way, shape or form, just at the moment.

Connie   It's all right. You just have to sit there and pass me things. I've got to decorate this Christmas tree. Here, grab this. *(She puts the box beside him.)*

Harry   *(peering inside the box).* Reminds me of when I used to decorate our tree at home. Ah, such happy times! That was when I *had* a home. *(Pathetically.)* Nowadays, I have to make do with the public tree in the precinct.

Connie   Stop it! You'll have me in tears in a minute!

Harry   Heartless wench!

Connie   Right! You got glass balls?

Harry   *(he does a 'double take').* I beg your pardon?

Connie   *(patiently).* In the *box*.

Harry   Oh, I see. *(He digs in the box and produces some glass globes.)* Here you are. And I do believe that one or two of them might still be in one piece.

Connie   Loads got broke last year. They make tempting targets for anyone with a hooligan streak.

Harry   Then why bother, if all your efforts are to be rendered futile?

Connie   You have to keep trying, don't you? You can't give in to them. That'd be giving in to anarchy. *(She busies herself at the tree, with Harry handing over various objects to her.)*

Harry   Well, it's refreshing to find someone who still has hope for the human race. Er, I know it's probably politically incorrect to say it – and I know it's a cliché – but what *is* a nice girl like you doing in a job like this?

Connie   It's what's called 'earning a living'. Something which you obviously know little about.

Harry   I shall treat that with the contempt it deserves. I happen to have been in employment most of my life. What I meant was, surely there's something less… less *masculine* you could do?

Connie   You call decorating a Christmas tree 'masculine'?

Harry   I was rather meaning your role as keeper of the keys.

Connie   It's all right, is this. There's usually nothing to it at night. I just have to make sure everything's locked and bolted, keep awake, and call the police if there's any major trouble. To tell you the truth, the main problem is boredom – trying to keep from nodding off between rounds. That's why I volunteered to decorate the tree, to pass a bit of time.

Harry   But surely Tollerbay Shopping Centre isn't the extent of your ambitions, is it?

Connie   God no! Oh, I had my dreams of greatness, like everyone else when they're young. Only my ambitions took a back seat when Jamie came along. He's my son – seven years old now, and lovely with it. *(She digs in her jacket pocket.)* Here, I've got a photo. *(She hands it over.)*

Harry   Cute little fellow. So you're married then? *(He hands photo back.)*

Connie   You do come from the Stone Age, don't you? Being married isn't a requirement for having kids, you know! These things tend to happen. To tell the truth, I couldn't even say where his father is at the moment. Not that I care. Haven't set eyes on him since the day I told him I was pregnant. He took off then, and he's probably still running.

Harry   I see. Hence the need for ready cash. But where is the boy at this moment?

Connie   Mum looks after him while I'm working. Coincidentally enough, *she* was deserted around the time she was expecting *me*. And would you believe that the exact same thing happened to her mother? I reckon it must be a family trait to attract the itinerant sods of this world! Any tinsel?

(Harry hands some strands of tinsel to her.)

Harry   So what did you want to do with your life?

Connie Daft idea really, but... now, don't you dare laugh... well, I always wanted to be an actress – stage, mind, not tele' or films. I do some stuff with a local amateur drama group, and I love it. Not that I'm any Judy Dench, you understand. I met Don – Jamie's father – through the group. He thought he was a wonderful actor. Well, I suppose he did manage to fool *me* all right!

Harry   So, you are now claiming that you are interested in theatre.

Connie 'Course I am! I go as often as I can afford it to see the professional productions.

Harry   Then I cannot for the life of me understand why you haven't yet recognised me. Go on, take a good look.

(Connie peers closely at him. She puts a finger to her lips, as though thinking hard, then points at him, as though she has spotted something familiar.)

Connie You're... now, don't tell me...

Harry   *(eagerly).* Yes?

Connie *(dropping her hand).* No, that's not it.

Harry   Oh, *do* come on! It's not that hard!

Connie You're not...? *(With mounting excitement.)* Surely, you can't be...?

Harry   *(eagerly).* Yes? *Yes?*

Connie You're not Daniel Day Lewis, fallen on hard times, are you?

Harry   Who on earth is Daniel Day Lewis? Take another look. *(He stands, the 'leg problem' seemingly having disappeared, and strikes a pose, hands on hips, a typical 'pantomime dame' pose.)* Hang on. *(He removes the hat.)* How about now?

Connie You trying to tell me something, standing like that?

Harry   Harry Hollingsworth! *(Blank response from Connie.)* Hollingsworth! It is my stage name, of course. And you mean you've never heard of me? *(With extravagant stage gestures.)* Ah, how fleeting is fame! How transient is glory! How...

Connie How many times have I to tell you that you've got to leave? Especially as your legs seem to have made a sudden miraculous recovery!

(Harry suddenly realises his mistake and his legs buckle as he hobbles back to the bench and sits down.)

Harry   You don't believe I'm in show business?

Connie Damn right I do! From what I've just seen, you're definitely an accomplished actor! So, how about exiting stage left? *(She points.)*

Harry A brief pause, I beg you, while I struggle to regain my strength. My ten minutes grace is still not up.

Connie Oh, all right. You've got another three minutes – not one second more.

Harry Why are the young so dominated by time? Still, I suppose I used to be the same. Trying to pack as much as I could into every single day. That was until time started to dictate to *me* instead.

Connie What branch of showbiz were you in then? Before you started living al fresco, as it were?

Harry I was... *am* an entertainer.

Connie A busker, are you? I haven't seen you in the precinct.

Harry *(insulted).* I am *not* a busker! I'll have you know, I have been employed in some of the most prestigious theatres in England.

Connie 'Course! You were stage doorman!

Harry My dear girl, I have been top of many a music hall bill. Happy Harry Hollingsworth, the people's comedian. No programme was complete without my scintillating stories, my jovial jocularity, my...

Connie ...tedious tales?

Harry I would appreciate it if you would cease ending my sentences. I was going to say, my rapturous repartee.

Connie What's that when it's at home?

Harry Do you know nothing, child? The use of big words to introduce an act in music hall is traditional.

Connie Isn't music hall like... the good old days?

Harry It is known under that title.

Connie With the accent on 'old' – as in 'past', 'long gone', 'historical', 'defunct'. A bit like you.

Harry I'll have you know, at this time of year, Christmas, I was especially in demand.

Connie Don't tell me! You were Santa Claus in his grotty!

Harry I believe the word is 'grotto'.

Connie Looking at the state of you, *I'm* closer the mark!

Harry Do you mind! I was a rather splendid Dame!

Connie Have a sex change, did you?

Harry *(sighing).* The Dame in *pantomime*. I was acknowledged among my peers as being one of the finest in the history of the art. My Widow Twankey had them rolling in the aisles.

Connie   You want to keep it covered up then, don't you?

Harry   How little significance all this has to young people today with their nightclubs and satellite television.

Connie   Now, that's where you're wrong, Mr Happy Harry. I happen to like panto, as does Jamie. So don't you go lumping all young people together!

Harry   I wasn't to know, was I?

Connie   There's a lot you don't know about me. Right then! *(She steps back to look at the tree.)* That's looking a bit better. I expect it'll be stripped before the day's out, but at least I tried. Are you feeling fit enough to trot off now?

Harry   *(sighing).* I haven't 'trotted' for years. I do recall my success as *Dame* Trot in... But, if you insist, I will reluctantly leave. And I hope you feel suitably ashamed at the way you are treating a respected member of the theatrical community.

Connie   Oh, yeah! I'm dead ashamed! Now, on yer bike!

Harry   *(standing).* I don't ride a bike. It was a skill I never learnt in my youth, even though I was the first person ever to attempt to pilot a unicycle across the stage of the London Palladium.

Connie   Hang on – you mean the *real* London Palladium?

Harry   To the best of my knowledge there is only the one. Oh yes, it's true. The only trouble was, I was the first to ride it *off* the stage too. I underestimated the space I required, and ended up in the orchestra pit with my pride mangled and my trousers sadly rent asunder.

Connie   *(admiringly).* The London Palladium! Imagine!

Harry   I've played 'em all in my time, my dear. Some venues were pretty difficult, I can tell you. But Harry Hollingsworth was an acknowledged master at wooing an audience! *(He sighs.)* Ah well, sadly it is now time to take my final bow in this establishment, and move on I know not where. *(He stands and goes to pick up his bags.)*

Connie   Hold on a minute. Not so fast.
(Harry promptly drops his bags, sits down, and beams at her.)

Harry   I knew that underneath that rather large jacket beats a heart of pure gold!

Connie   You're still leaving. But before you go, these fairy lights need untangling. And I'd, er, I'd like to ask you something.

Harry   Fire away, young lady! I am all ears – the unfortunate result of being forced to wear my cap pulled right down when I was a child. My mother has a lot to answer for.

Connie *(sitting beside him).* It's just that... well, I could do with some advice... about going professional. I was wondering... how you got your first break?

Harry *(taking out the lights set from the box).* Fell downstairs as a mere child, dear girl. Took ages for the leg to heal.

Connie Break into *show business*, you comedian!

Harry It's so long ago, I can hardly recall...

Connie *(standing).* In that case, you'd best be going.

Harry *(hastily).* But now I come to think of it... *(Connie and Harry untangle the lights between them.)* I was a mere youth. Good heavens! It must have been over fifty-five years ago.

Connie Don't tell me you were a war hero into the bargain!

Harry Do you mind! I'm not that old! I was sixteen when the war ended. It was a desperate time – people were looking for something to cheer them up.

Connie And along came Happy Harry!

Harry I was born to it. My father and mother were in the business. Father was a Pierrot and Mother used to sell the tickets to the shows. *(In answer to her blank look.)* Don't tell me you've never heard of Pierrots - entertainers who dressed up in black and white costumes and performed on the sands at seaside resorts. It meant that I was involved in showbiz from a very early age.

Connie So did you become a Pierrot then?

Harry Oh, the Pierrots had all gone by that time. Music Hall was popular, though, and young comics were in short supply. *(He stands and moves slowly forward.)* I started in this very town. At the old Palace. Every week had a different programme, and talk about variety! There was a ventriloquist, a light opera singer, a couple who played xylophones, an illusionist, beautiful chorus girls, and, of course, Sheila and her performing poodles. We all hated going on after her. You never knew what you might step in. And then there was me – Harry Hollingsworth, comic interjections.

Connie So how come you ended up at Christmas time dressing up as a big fat woman in a daft wig?

Harry Mainly the fact that the pay in those days was lousy. We had to work all year round to keep body and soul together.

Connie Tell me about it! You don't think this is my idea of fun, do you? Working right up to Christmas?

Harry But I have to admit I never really regarded pantomime as work. It was so enjoyable. And the faces of the children, and the way they joined in the fun... worth it just for that alone. *(He sits again.)*

Connie So there you are – summer spent at the seaside, winter pretending to be a female. Sounds idyllic to me.

Harry It was – until Cliff Richard came along.

Connie Oh, come on! I know some people don't like his singing, but I can't believe he wiped out the tradition of pantomime single-handed.

Harry He wasn't alone. Pop music was becoming all the rage. So the promoters decided that what audiences wanted was their favourite pop stars on stage. Out went Harry Hollingsworth – in came Cliff Richard and the Shadows.

Connie You didn't stand a chance!

Harry True, my dear, so very true. And with no work, the income dried up.

Connie Did you have a family?

Harry Yes. But I'd only been married a short time when it all went wrong. We waited to wed in those days till we earned enough to support our wives. And not long after there was another mouth to feed, our daughter. Still, financially, we were breaking even for a time. Until Sir Cliff and his ilk put the kybosh on it all.

Connie So what happened to your wife? You mean she left you because you because you didn't earn enough?

Harry She came from a family background where convention had it that the man should bring in a steady wage, while the woman looked after home and children. Her father convinced her that dragging around the theatrical circuit, living in cheap digs, was no way to bring up a child. We drifted apart. I haven't seen her in years.

Connie *(drapes the lights over the tree.)* What about your daughter?

Harry The same. I doubt I'd even recognise her if I bumped into her. I don't even know if they still live in this town – in this *country*! Look, I've just realised something. I'm entirely the wrong person to ask for advice. Just take a look at how *I've* ended up!

Connie But at least you were famous once.

Harry That was so long ago, most of my audiences have long since passed on! I did get another crack at it in the eighties when some theatres brought back traditional panto. But it was never the same.

Connie My Jamie loves traditional panto.

Harry Nice to know there are discerning children still about.

Connie   He's never gone for the ones with soap stars or big names. He just likes the slapstick.

Harry   As do all kids.

Connie   Only, Jamie likes it more than most. *(She sits beside him.)* You see, he's… well, he's a bit backward at coming forward, that's how Mam describes it. He has difficulty… learning things. He's just a bit… slow, that's all. But he's a lovely kiddie, really he is! Real affectionate, and…

Harry   I don't doubt it for a moment.

Connie   But one thing he does react to is physical humour. He's not so hot on the corny jokes. But it does my heart good to hear him laughing at the daft antics. *(She stands and continues dressing the tree.)* I used to take him regularly to the panto at the Opera House here. He just loved those silly routines, you know, the ghost being chased off by the Dame, the stunt with broken crockery. But then, last year, for the first time for ages, there wasn't a panto. Jamie was gutted.

Harry   Too expensive to put on, so I heard on the grapevine.

Connie   And there isn't going to be one this year either.

Harry   I could hazard a guess and say that professional panto in this town is as good as dead.

Connie   But I reckon there's still a demand. Look – supposing the actors didn't need paying?

Harry   Oh, come on! Even actors have to *eat*!

Connie   What if there were enough amateurs in town interested in putting on a panto? And what if we were able to hire a theatre at a reasonable cost?

Harry   But even so…

Connie   I'm sure I could raise a cast if I put my mind to it. There's bags of enthusiasm in our group, believe me. But enthusiasm isn't enough on its own. To guarantee success, we'd need someone to direct it – someone with loads of experience. If possible, a retired professional, and, preferably, someone who could also play the Dame. Someone like the great Harry Hollingsworth, perhaps?

Harry   My dear girl! The idea's ridiculous!

Connie   Why is it ridiculous?

Harry   Because… because, for one thing, it's *years* since I trod the boards. I'm out of practise. And, as you well know, my poor old legs aren't what they were.

Connie   Only because you rely too much on this stuff. *(She kicks the* *wine bottle. She starts to pack Harry's belongings into carriers.)*

Harry   No, I'm sorry. I'm not saying it isn't a good idea, and I wish you every success. But as for me… well, it's out of the question! I'm afraid you'll have to look elsewhere. Now, I really must be going. You've kept me here *far* too long already. *(He stands. From his pocket, he takes a pair of purple gloves and carefully puts them on, with a great show.)*

Connie   *(slowly).* I don't believe this! This is *so* weird!

Harry   *(affronted).* And what is wrong with purple gloves, pray? I happen to like the colour. Well, to tell the truth, someone threw them away and I am just recycling them. I didn't pinch them!

Connie   Who would pinch gloves that colour? No, it's just one of those coincidences you come across all the time in life.

Harry   Ah! You also wear purple gloves?

Connie   Not on your life! No, it's just… Do you know that song that always gets trotted out at Christmas? You know – a partridge in a pear tree?

Harry   Naturally I know it.

Connie   A few years back, there was a panto… I've forgotten which one. Anyway, the Dame and his stooges did a parody of that rhyme. You know, with daft things substituting for the real stuff in the song.

Harry   Are we getting to the point of this story, or should I sit down again?

Connie   Well, I don't remember all of them, of course, but I do recall that instead of two turtle doves, they sang about *two purple gloves. (Peering at him.)* Here! It wasn't you underneath all that grotesque makeup, was it?

Harry   Not if it was fairly recent. I haven't worked this town for a long, long time.

Connie   Anyway, Jamie loved that song so much that he made me go through it with him afterwards – as much as I could remember of it anyway.

Harry   It would be interesting to know where you got the leaping lords, not to mention the drummers drumming. I bet the neighbours complained!

Connie   No, you idiot! We substituted things we found around the house. You know – leaping lords, ironing boards, that sort of thing. But the one bit he always remembered from the original was two purple gloves. And here you are, wearing purple gloves!

Harry   Fascinating. Now, will you kindly unlock the outer door for me?

	Otherwise I shall have to take the gloves off again, or I won't feel the benefit when I go out into the cold, cold snow!
Connie	And you won't reconsider – about the pantomime?
Harry	Like I said, it's all too long ago. That part of my life is finished, done with, at an end…
Connie	OK, I get the point! It was just a thought. Right, I'll let you out then.
Harry	Anyway, there's no script. And what about a support crew? You'll need lighting and sound, backstage, front of house, props, costumes! The list is endless.
Connie	I thought problems were made to be overcome? I thought people of your generation didn't know the meaning of giving in? My grandmother always claimed there was no such word as 'can't'. You oldies always go on about how young people today are all just idle spongers. Yet when you're faced with someone like me, someone willing to have a go at something creative, you're suddenly too old to bother! Look, as far as a script goes, I happen to have a load in the attic – been there years. Someone must have bought them as a job lot from a jumble sale and hadn't the heart to throw them away. I reckon we could probably find something worth doing among them.
Harry	Yes, but even so… I really don't think…
Connie	Fine. There's no more to be said then. You go back to starring in your one-man show in your cold, dark, damp doorway. Nobody'll mind. Nobody'll miss you. Nobody'll *care*. Especially not Connie Callavino.
Harry	Callavino? I thought your name was Franklin?
Connie	That was my father's name. Connie Callavino is going to be my stage name. It was my grandmother's maiden name. She was from Italy originally, you know. I just thought it sounded more showbiz than 'Franklin'.
Harry	Er, yes… it certainly does. *(He hesitates.)*
Connie	OK. This way, Mr Hollingsworth.
Harry	Just a minute. I've been thinking.
Connie	It's too late for that now. I'm off on my rounds in a minute. Anyway, I've lost heart.
Harry	What if I were to say I'd do it?
Connie	I'd wonder what made you change your mind so suddenly.
Harry	Let's just say it was hearing a name from the past…
Connie	Don't say you've started hearing things now!
Harry	Perhaps it is about time I did something creative.

Connie   Attaboy, Harry! That is, if you really mean it.

Harry   Young lady, Harry Hollingsworth's word is his bond. Of *course* I mean it. Tell you what, I'll do it for your Jamie.

Connie   Great! He'll be so chuffed! Look, give me your address and we'll arrange to meet and discuss it. Oh, I forgot. You're of no fixed abode at the moment, aren't you?

Harry   Why don't we start the planning right now? I'll hazard a guess that you'll find 'Jack and the Beanstalk' among those scripts you mentioned. That always goes down well.

Connie   How do you know that particular script'll be among the collection? *(Realising.)* Oh, I suppose it's *bound* to be there because it's so popular.

Harry   But I'll only be Dame if you're principal boy. Of course, you'll have to dress up a little.

Connie   Yeah, I will – when we buy the costumes.

Harry   My dear girl, are you made of money? Have you never heard of improvisation? What have you got on under your jacket? Take it off and show me! *(He pulls at her jacket. Connie backs away.)*

Connie   Here! What you on about? You're not thinking of trying it on, are you?

Harry   My dear girl, at my age, I've forgotten what that phrase refers to!

(Connie takes off her jacket to reveal a white t-shirt underneath. This should be decorated with a colourful logo or picture. She takes pieces of leftover tinsel and wraps them around her head and waist. She pirouettes in front of Harry.)

Connie   How do I look?

Harry   Lovely! *(Pause.)* Or should I say 'Bellissimo!'?

(Connie looks at him strangely, but Harry turns away and rummages in the carrier bags and produces various items. He takes the coloured sheet. This should have a pre-prepared hole cut centrally so Harry can slip it over his head as a frock. He goes and gets the mop and removes the handle to use the head as a wig. Again, this can be pre-prepared with some strands cut away to reveal his face, and a length of elastic which Harry can slip under his chin to hold it on. A string of coloured plastic beads from the decorations box hung around his neck completes the picture. Connie uses a lipstick from her pocket to rouge his cheeks. She switches on the Christmas tree fairy lights. Coloured stage lighting should now be brought in to add to the theatrical effect.)

Connie   OK. So we've managed to transform ourselves into complete idiots – admittedly at no cost. What do we do now?

Harry   How about that song you were talking about earlier? You know? Two purple gloves? It'd make a great finale.

Connie   I don't know if I can remember it.

Harry   Oh, I know it – only too well!

Connie   You start it off. And start from six. I haven't got all night!
(As they go through the song they substitute for the proper items mentioned in the song various items from among Harry's things or from the area around them.)

Harry   *(singing).* On the sixth day of Christmas, my true love sent to me – six... *(he produces a pullover)* ...jumpers fraying!

Connie   Five... *(She kicks the dustbin.)* ...old bins!

Harry   Four...*(Pointing to the stationer's shop sign at rear.)* ...drawing boards.

Connie   Three... *(From her pocket or the box..)* ...felt pens!

Harry   Two... *(Holding them up.)* ...purple gloves!

Connie   And a... *(She looks around.)*
(Harry produces a sandwich from his carrier and gives it to her. She turns it diagonally and fixes it, like a star, at the top of the tree.)

Harry/Connie ...sandwich in a fir tree!
(At the end of the song, they take a bow and go into an involuntary hug, which they break from with some embarrassment. At that moment, Connie's radio crackles into life.)

GEOFF   *(over radio).* Connie? What the hell is going on down there? Why are you dressed like that? And who's that with you? Good God, woman! Have you been at the booze? I know it's Christmas but... I hope you realise you're turning this security lark into a *bloody pantomime*!
(Connie and Harry go into hoots of laughter and hug each other. The lights fade and a lively Christmas carol is played as the Curtain closes.)

END

Properties

Main set Bench L of C. Artificial Christmas tree DR. Litterbin UC. Mop and bucket UL. Carrier bags containing coloureds sheet, sunglasses, pullover, sandwich, plus some extra clothing.
Offstage (for Connie) Cardboard box containing Christmas tree decorations, fairy lights, tinsel.

Personal

Connie Walkie-talkie, torch, badge. In jacket pocket, felt tip pen, photograph.
Harry Hat, mackintosh. In pocket of mac, pair of purple gloves.

Lighting

Play opens in darkness, with faint background green glow.
Full lighting *cue* **Connie** And you've probably blinded me for life!
Finale, coloured lighting on area of bench.
Fade to black at end.

Sound effects

Cheerful Christmas carol at beginning and end (e.g. 'Deck the halls').
Final speech by Geoff is played over PA system.

The only
monthly magazine
passionate
about
amateur theatre